For Marielle

COURGETTE

Christopher Trotter

Photography by Caroline Trotter

2 w in a series!

Christopher Trotter

© Christopher Trotter 2014

Published by Momentum publishing.

A CIP catalogue record for this book is available from the British Library.

ISBN 978-0-9926830-1-6

Produced by Print & Design, University of St Andrews
Website: www.st-andrews.ac.uk/printanddesign

Printed by Latimer Trend & Company Limited

Distributed by Christopher Trotter
Tel: 07739049639

CONTENTS

Introduction 5

The Nutritional Value
of Courgette 7

Buying and Storing 9

Cooking 9

Grilled Courgettes with
Tomato and Bean Salad 11

Tempura Style Deep Fried
Courgettes 13

Courgette Roulade 15

Courgette and Haloumi
Cake with Roast Red
Peppers 17

Courgette and
Coriander Tart 19

Squash and
Courgette Stew 21

Courgette Spaghetti
with Avocado 23

Courgette and Apricot
Hummus 25

Courgette Lasagne 27

Timbale of Courgette
with Wild Garlic Pesto 29

Courgette Soup 31

Courgette Tian 33

Chocolate Courgette
Cake 35

Ratatouille 37

Summer Vegetable Stew 39

Courgette Soup with
Rosemary and St Andrews
Farmhouse Cheese Croute . . . 41

Chilled Courgette Soup
with Dill 43

Courgette Chutney 45

Courgette Flowers
stuffed with Mozzarella
and Anchovies 47

Shredded Courgette 49

Courgette and Cabbage
Crumble 51

Tomato and Courgette
Salad with Cumin 53

Courgettes Skewered with
Lemon and Chicken 55

Round Courgettes stuffed
with Red Rice and
Vegetables 57

Courgette Frittata 59

Sweet and Sour
Pickled Courgettes 61

Marinated Courgette Salad . . 63

Crab and Courgette Bake 65

Herb Tabouleh with
Roasted Courgettes 67

Courgette Muffins 69

Biographies 70

Acknowledgements 71

St Andrews Cheese 72

INTRODUCTION

In this our second book of vegetables, I have chosen the courgette as it's a summer vegetable and it's the summer I have chosen to publish. My memories of courgettes are based round the family table in St. Andrews where my mother, a superb organic gardener never stopped trying new things, and I can remember the huge ungainly plants with their vast slightly coarse leaves spreading out like some alien being. After the leaves the first protrusions would be the beautiful orange flower which then withered and the actual fruit itself emerged, a tiny pinky sized pale green, which in the blink of an eye was a few inches long. And then there were the escapees which, growing unnoticed beneath the foliage could emerge marrow like in a matter of days, these my mum would stuff with mince, but try my recipe with rice and herbs on page 57. Otherwise just snapped off and eaten there and then they had a delightful crunch and delicate flavour which is properly revealed with light cooking or being mixed in a salad with good oil and lemon juice.

The humble courgette, or Zucchini depending where you come from, is such a versatile vegetable I could have given a recipe for stewing them in butter and mixing the resulting purée with white sauce and rice and browned in the oven from Elizabeth David's "An Omelette and a glass of wine" or Darina Allens's simple salad with olive oil and sea salt, but the cognoscenti will already know these. So I have chosen ideas based around technique and using other ingredients which are also in season at the same time. For when does one need a book with 30 Courgette recipes most? When there is a glut in the garden or they are cheap in the shops or make up half your veg box!

Courgettes come in all shapes, sizes and colours but never mistake them for marrows, which are a different vegetable all together and outsized courgettes are not marrows. Unfortunately many chefs seem to think that really tiny courgettes are what to look for, but this is mainly because they look pretty, whole, on a plate but in fact a mature tasting courgette needs to be about 12-17 cm in length. My guru on these matters is Guy Watson from Riverford Farm and he works on two sowings a year. The first under glass in April and then planting direct in June which gives them a harvest of courgettes right through to the first frosts in autumn which will kill off a plant. They can be very prolific with two or three plants producing plenty of courgettes day after day for several weeks.

THE NUTRITIONAL VALUE OF COURGETTE

Like any vegetable the fresher it is, the better the health giving qualities, so bought locally from a farmers market, farm shop or good greengrocer. By buying and using fresh seasonal produce you are also helping the local economy. Flavour will also fade with time, which is why many veg box businesses don't put courgettes in them as by the time they get to their destination and they hang about for a while they loose their goodness, so buy often and use quickly! Just think how long ago a courgette from outwith the UK has been picked!

Courgettes are low in calories, with only about 17 per 100g, they have no saturated fat or cholesterol. The skin is a good source of fibre which helps to prevent constipation as well as offering some protection against bowel cancers. Therefore they are good for those people looking for weight and cholesterol control.

The golden skin varieties are rich in Flavanoid poly-phenolic antioxidants which help to reduce oxygen derived free radicals. Free radicals have an ageing effect on our bodies, so always eat the skin, trimming away any marked bits of bruised flesh.

Courgettes have a moderate source of folates providing 6% RDA per 100g , which are good for pregnant women. Courgettes are a good source of potassium which is good for the heart and helps reduce blood pressure. They are rich in Vitamin A and Vitamin C.

Courgettes also contain moderate amounts of the Vitamin B group such as thiamin, pyridoxine and riboflavin. They also contain minerals like iron, manganese, phosphorus and zinc.

GRILLED COURGETTES WITH TOMATO AND BEAN SALAD

The cooking method here can be used for various other dishes mentioned in the book which will refer back to grilling, but I am just giving a recipe to go with it as well! Grilled slice courgettes are great on a barbecue along with peppers to add to your grilled meats.

INGREDIENTS

400g can of cannelloni beans, drained
3 tblsp extra virgin olive oil
4 courgettes
12 cherry tomatoes cut in half
Sea salt and freshly ground black pepper

Sorrel dressing:
Handful of sorrel leaves
1 clove garlic
100ml olive oil
¼ tsp sea salt

METHOD

1   Whiz all the dressing ingredients together in a food processor.
2   Mix the beans together with the cherry tomatoes and the dressing.
3   Top and tail the courgettes and slice them into thick ribbons. Brush with olive oil and grill on a ribbed pan or barbecue.
4   Dress on a plate and dollop the dressed bean and tomato mix on top.

TEMPURA STYLE DEEP FRIED COURGETTES

A really simple way to cook them is to dip in a batter and then deep fry like chips. Smaller firm ones are best so that the middles are not too soft, you can even deep fry small ones with the flower still attached.

INGREDIENTS

150g plain flour
2 tblsp rapeseed oil
Splash tepid water
2 egg whites
Salt and freshly ground black pepper
Coarse salt

METHOD

1   Mix the flour and oil together and then mix in enough tepid water to form a texture like double cream. Leave to rest for 20 minutes.
2   Heat the oil in a fryer or in a large open pan.
3   Cut the courgettes into chip shapes.
4   Add a pinch of salt to the egg whites and whisk until they just form light peaks, fold into the batter, season with black pepper.
5   Dip the courgettes pieces in to the batter and fry until light brown.
6   Dry on kitchen paper and eat immediately sprinkled with some coarse salt.

COURGETTE ROULADE

A simple dish to make and then easy to fill with whatever you fancy. I have served it warm with a creamy mushroom filling, but here I have made a crème fraiche and roast red pepper filling, the important thing to remember is to really squeeze the moisture out of the grated courgette and look for colour in the filling, hence the flecks of red pepper here. It's good as a first course or as a lunch dish with a salad.

INGREDIENTS

500g courgettes (grated weight)
1 tblsp vegetable oil
1 onion, peeled and finely chopped
Salt and freshly ground black pepper
3 eggs separated

For the filling:
1 red pepper
150ml crème fraiche

METHOD

1   Turn the oven to 375C gas mark 6.
2   Line a 30x23 cm baking tray with cling film.
3   Top and tail and grate the courgettes (you need 500g prepared weight).
4   In a large frying pan, sweat the onion in the oil, until soft, but do not colour.
5   Squeeze out the courgette and add to the pan and cook over a medium heat to soften and dry out a little, season with the salt and pepper and set aside to cool.
6   Whisk the egg whites until just holding, mix the yolks into the courgette mixture and then fold a little of the whites into it to mix through then gently fold the courgette mix back in to the whites to form a light mixture.
7   Spread carefully into the prepared tin and bake in the oven for 20 minutes until lightly coloured and just firm. Turn out onto a sheet of greaseproof and allow to cool.
8   Cut the pepper in half and scoop out the seeds, make slashes on the sides and brush with olive oil. Increase the oven to 400 gas 6 and roast for half an hour, allow to cool peel off the skin and chop into small dice. Mix with the crème Fraiche.
9   Spread the mixture over the roulade and roll up.

COURGETTE AND HALOUMI CAKE WITH ROAST RED PEPPERS

An unusual idea I got from lunch at the Gallery of Modern Art in Edinburgh, the roast red peppers are cooked as in the roulade recipe (page 15) but there is no need to peel or chop them up.

INGREDIENTS

300g courgettes (grated weight)
1 onion finely chopped
250g haloumi cheese
75 g plain flour
Zest of a lemon
2 eggs
2 tblsp chopped dill
Olive oil
Roast red peppers

METHOD

1   Coarsely grate the courgettes, and squeeze out thoroughly.
2   Combine with the onion, haloumi, flour, lemon zest, eggs and dill.
3   Form into small patties and leave to firm up for half an hour.
4   Fry in hot oil until golden brown on both sides.

Serve with the roast peppers.

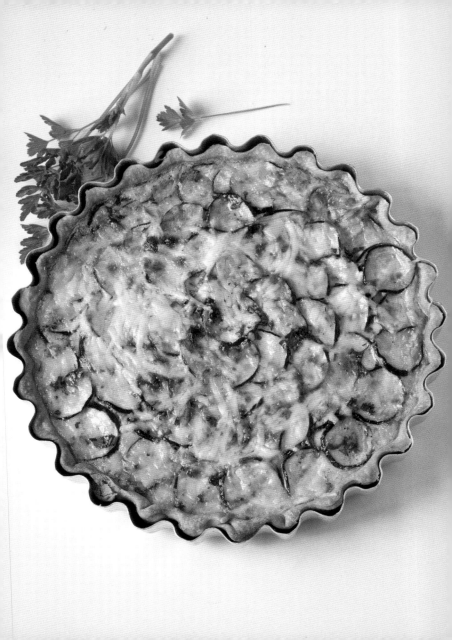

COURGETTE AND CORIANDER TART

Great as a first course or a light lunch dish, it's important to really rinse the sliced courgettes after salting to properly remove that flavour and don't season with salt! Coriander is good with this but do try other herbs, dill for instance.

INGREDIENTS

Shortcrust pastry
800g small courgettes
Salt and freshly ground black pepper
3 tblsp rapeseed oil
2 eggs and 2 egg yolks
300ml double cream
2 tblsp fresh coriander
2 tblsp grated Anster or St Andrews farmhouse cheese

METHOD

1   Preheat the oven to 190C gas mark 5.
2   Line a 22 cm baking tin with the pastry and bake blind for
    15 minutes.
3   Slice the courgettes into thin rounds and layer in a colander,
    sprinkling salt on each layer. Leave for 30 minutes, rinse thoroughly
    under a cold tap and drain on kitchen paper.
4   Heat the oil in a large heavy based pan and lightly fry the courgettes
    to soften but not to colour, remove from the pan and drain.
5   Whisk the eggs, yolks and cream with some pepper, tear up the
    coriander leaves and mix with the courgettes and spread over the
    base of the pastry case.
6   Pour over the egg mixture, sprinkle over the cheese and bake until
    just set, about 30 minutes.

Delicious with a tomato and olive oil salad.

SQUASH AND COURGETTE STEW

You can also use marrow in this. It is a simple dish to make and like most spiced dishes tastes better the next day as the flavours are allowed to develop, do play around with the spices you may prefer more or less cayenne.

INGREDIENTS

1 tblsp olive oil,
1 large onion, peeled and chopped
3 cloves garlic crushed with a little salt
1 tsp ground ginger
1 tsp turmeric
1 tsp cayenne
1 tsp harissa, sauce
600g squash cut into chunks
500g courgettes cut into chunks
500ml vegetable stock
Pinch saffron (optional)
4 tblsp raisins
2 tsp honey
2 tblsp chopped coriander

METHOD

1   Take a large frying pan and soften the onion in it with the oil.
2   Stir in the garlic and spices and cook, stirring gently for 5 minutes.
3   Stir in the squash and courgettes to coat with the spice mixture.
4   Add the stock, saffron, if using, raisins and honey and simmer for 10 minutes until vegetables are just cooked, and the liquid should form a thickish sauce.
5   Stir in the coriander and serve with rice.

COURGETTE SPAGHETTI WITH AVOCADO

Preparing courgettes in this manner gives you scope for all sorts of accompanying ideas, so do try this one and then use your imagination, lots of fresh herbs and perhaps some grated Anster cheese . . .

INGREDIENTS

4 medium courgettes
15 Brazil nuts
3 avocados
4 tblsp rapeseed oil
Juice of a lime
½ tsp salt
20 button mushrooms

METHOD

1   You can cut the courgettes by hand, trim top and bottom then slice along the length carefully into four slices, then slice them into long strips. Some food processors have a blade for this but make sure the courgettes are firm other wise you may end up with a mush! I use a wonderful gadget called a Mandolin which does the job very quickly.

2   Put the nuts in a food processor and blend for about 5 minutes, until smooth, add the avocados, 2 tblsp oil and salt, add a little cold water until a creamy consistency is achieved.

3   Slice the mushrooms, heat the remaining oil in a large pan and gently sweat the mushrooms to soften, add the courgette spaghetti and stir to soften for a few minutes, pour on the sauce and mix to heat through. Don't allow to get too hot as the avocado will turn bitter.

COURGETTE AND APRICOT HUMMUS

A lovely alternative to chick pea hummus, the apricots provide a delicate sweetness and the pomegranate molasses adds a touch of the east. I first came across it in Syria a few years back at a road side stall, I wasn't sure what it was but as it was being sold everywhere, I thought I had better give it a try!

INGREDIENTS

20g dried apricots
2 tblsp lemon juice
7 tblsp rapeseed oil
1 large courgette
1 clove garlic
Pinch sea salt
Ground black pepper
1 tsp Pomegranate molasses
½ tsp cumin

METHOD

1 Blitz the apricots with the oil and lemon juice in a food processor, for two minutes.
2 Add the remaining ingredients and process until smooth.

COURGETTE LASAGNE

This dish really uses sliced courgettes in place of pasta sheets, but again you could replace aubergines with the courgettes for a moussaka or try using a thick tomato sauce in place of the traditional mince or ragu for a vegetarian alternative.

INGREDIENTS

450g cooked mince or ragu sauce
5 courgettes
50g butter
15g plain flour
560ml milk
120g Anster or St Andrews Farmhouse cheese

METHOD

1   Turn the oven to 200C gas mark 6.
2   Make a white sauce with the butter, flour and milk.
3   Pour a third of the white sauce on the base of a large dish, then add a layer of courgette slices, about half of what you have, then sprinkle on a third of the cheese, then top with half the mince.
4   Repeat, finishing with the remaining white sauce and sprinkle over the remaining cheese.
5   Bake in the oven until browned and bubbling, about 30 minutes.

TIMBALE OF COURGETTE WITH WILD GARLIC PESTO

A really lovely idea from my friend and great cook Alison Sykora (you can also use basil pesto but I like to promote our son's products!). It makes a very attractive first course – Thanks Alison! A timbale is a moulded dish and can be made either in a small timbale or metal mould or use a dariole (which is similar) or a ramekin.

INGREDIENTS

3 courgettes
4 dsp Trotter's Wild Garlic Pesto
50g St Andrews Farmhouse cheese
Oil for lining moulds

METHOD

1   Preheat oven to 180C gas mark 4.
2   Cut the courgettes into long thin strips and blanche in boiling salted water, until just slightly soft. Refresh in ice cold water, drain and dry thoroughly.
3   Cut the cheese into small chunks and mix with the pesto.
4   Grease four dariole moulds or ramekins with a little oil, line them with the courgette slices, making sure the sides are completely covered.
5   Dollop in the pesto mixture and fold over the slices to enclose, pressing down firmly and cover with cling film or greaseproof paper.
6   Cook in the oven for 20 minutes, allow to rest for 5 minutes and then turn out.

Serve with a salad and brown bread.

COURGETTE SOUP

I am indebted to the wonderful Brigid Allen for this superb soup and her skill at using large amounts of garlic and allowing vegetables to stew in either butter or oil for 10 to 15 minutes before adding liquids, it seems to enhance the flavours in the soups.

INGREDIENTS

1 onion, peeled and chopped
2 small carrots, peeled and chopped
2 tblsp olive oil
2 large courgettes topped and tailed and chopped
2 medium potatoes, chopped
4 cloves garlic
Coarse salt
2 tomatoes
550ml water
Several grinds black pepper

METHOD

1 In a heavy based lidded pan sweat the onions and carrots together over a low heat for about 15 minutes stirring occasionally to prevent colouring.
2 Stir in the courgettes and the potatoes.
3 Slice three of the garlic cloves and stir in, cover and cook gently for another 10 minutes.
4 Crush the remaining garlic clove with a teaspoon of the salt and add to the pan with the tomatoes and stir in for a few minutes.
5 Add the water and some black pepper and simmer for 20 minutes partially covered until soft. Leave to sit for 5 minutes before liquidising.

COURGETTE TIAN

I quite like the name Tian and although it is a Chinese word for the cosmos and a French cooking dish, here it's simply a layered dish! But perhaps because of the ingredients it is indeed a microcosm of the cosmos.

INGREDIENTS

3 tblsp olive oil
1 onion, peeled and chopped
2 cloves garlic crushed
500g courgettes, sliced
250g spinach, blanched and chopped
4 tblsp cooked brown rice
3 eggs beaten
50g cheese grated
1 tblsp bread crumbs
1 tblsp grated Anster cheese

METHOD

1   Preheat the oven to 180C gas mark 4.
2   Heat the oil in a frying pan and soften the onion.
3   Add the garlic, and add the courgettes and cook for 5 minutes stir in the spinach, and rice to heat through.
4   Remove from the heat and stir in the cheese and the beaten eggs season and then pour into a earthenware gratin dish.
5   Mix the breadcrumbs and cheese and sprinkle over.
6   Bake in the oven for 40 minutes.

CHOCOLATE COURGETTE CAKE

A very simple cake in which the vegetable simply disappears and provides moisture. It is a very good way of getting green vegetables into children (or adults!) who don't like them.

INGREDIENTS

180g plain chocolate 70%
200g plain flour
1 tsp baking powder
½ tsp bicarbonate of soda
½ tsp salt
125g caster sugar
2 large eggs lightly beaten
170ml vegetable oil
225g peeled courgettes (peeled weight) grated
60g chopped walnuts

METHOD

1   Line a deep 20 cm round tin.
2   Preheat oven to 180C gas mark 4.
3   Melt the chocolate in a bowl over a pan of hot water.
4   Sift the flour, baking powder, salt and sugar into a large bowl.
5   Beat the eggs into the oil and then mix in to the dry ingredients, add the chocolate and the courgettes, stir to combine well.
6   Add the nuts, pour into the tin and bake for about 50 minutes, leave in the tin for a few minutes before turning out to cool.

RATATOUILLE

To cook or not to cook, that is the question when it comes to this great dish and really it often depends on what you plan to use it for. Quickly cooked keeps colour and texture and makes a great first course, or accompaniment with other dishes. Likewise a piece of chicken quickly browned in a pan, then cooked for an hour buried in ratatouille is some thing else! Don't take the quantities too seriously it just gives you an idea of balance.

INGREDIENTS

450g onions
3 cloves garlic
(crushed with a little salt)
450g courgettes
450g red peppers
450g yellow peppers

450g aubergine
450g ripe tomatoes
Lots of olive oil
2 sprigs thyme
Handful basil
Salt and freshly ground black pepper

METHOD

1   Peel the onions and chop roughly.
2   Cut the courgettes in to 2 cm chunks.
3   Cut and de seed the peppers and cut into 2 cm chunks.
4   Cut the aubergine into 2 cm chunks.
5   De-stem and criss cross cut the tomatoes and blanche in boiling water, refresh in ice cold water, peel them cut them in quarters and remove the seeds (use these in a dressing).
6   Take a large frying pan and set the onions to soften in some olive oil for 10 minutes.
7   Take another pan, add olive oil and over a very high heat first colour the peppers and then add them to the onions then the aubergine and add to the onions, stir in the garlic.
8   Lastly colour the courgettes in the hot pan adding more oil as needed and stir in to the onion mixture, cook for another 5 minutes stir in the tomatoes and basil, heat through and serve.

SUMMER VEGETABLE STEW

I discovered Sybil Kapoor some years ago and have three of her excellent books. She is a great food writer and concentrates on flavours and textures. Admiration turned to adoration when through the auspices of Twitter I discovered she was a Moomintroll fan . . . This is borrowed from her.

INGREDIENTS

55g butter
4 quartered spring onions
1 crushed clove garlic
115g courgettes, cut in lengths
115g peas,
115g broad beans
2 little gem lettuces, quartered
1 tsp finely chopped tarragon
Salt and freshly ground black pepper

METHOD

1   Fry the onions and garlic gently in half the butter until soft.
2   Add the courgette, peas and beans, with a splash of water to help steam them. Season and cook gently for a few minutes.
3   Add the lettuce and allow to warm through, stir in the remaining butter and tarragon. Serve.

COURGETTE SOUP WITH ROSEMARY AND ST ANDREWS FARMHOUSE CHEESE CROUTE

Jane Stewart's cheese has great strength and depth of flavour, its seems a shame to waste any part of it, so like the Italians with Parmesan I use the rind from her cheese to add flavour, there is no stock in this soup the flavour comes from the cheese.

INGREDIENTS

3 tblsp olive oil
1 onion
(peeled and finely chopped)
1 kg courgettes chopped
3 cloves garlic crushed
Grated nutmeg
Salt and pepper
Sprig rosemary

30g rind from St Andrews
farmhouse cheese
550ml whole milk

6 slices of French loaf
(or other large crouton)
30g grated St Andrews
farmhouse cheese

METHOD

1   Heat the olive oil in a large pan over a low heat and sweat the onions until soft, about 7 minutes.
2   Add the chopped courgettes with the crushed garlic, a little nutmeg and some salt and pepper, stir in the rosemary and cheese rind, lower the heat and cover, leave for about 15 minutes stirring occasionally 'til the courgettes are soft.
3   Remove the rosemary and add the milk and allow to simmer for 5 minutes but not boil, then remove the rind and liquidise.

To serve the soup, brush the bread croutes with a little olive oil and toast briefly under a hot grill, turn over and sprinkle the cheese on top and melt briefly under the grill serve floating on top of the soup.

CHILLED COURGETTE SOUP WITH DILL

I make no apologies for having three soups in this book, they are all so different and each brings out a different character of the courgette, this chilled one is as good as a vichyssoise.

INGREDIENTS

700g courgettes
1 small onion, peeled and chopped
2 cloves garlic, crushed
1 tblsp olive oil
1.2 l stock
1 tsp corn flour
150ml Smetana or yoghurt or crème fraiche
2 tsp chopped fresh dill plus a few sprigs to garnish

METHOD

1   In a large pan, sweat off the onion until soft and add the garlic and courgettes, cook gently for 5 minutes.
2   Add the stock, simmer for 15 minutes until the courgettes are soft.
3   Slake the cornflour in a little cold water and stir in, simmer for another 5 minutes to cook out the floury flavour.
4   Cool slightly and stir in the Smetana and the dill, liquidise and chill.
5   Serve with a blob of the Smetana and a small sprig of dill.

COURGETTE CHUTNEY

A perfect late season's chutney a glut of courgette, some unripened tomatoes and some windfall apples, classic chutney ingredients.

INGREDIENTS

1 kg large courgette, diced
1 kg green tomatoes
500g cooking apples peeled cored and diced
500g raisins
500g dark brown sugar
600ml vinegar
½ tsp salt
1 tsp freshly ground black pepper
½ tsp ground coriander
Small piece ginger peeled and finely chopped
Small onion studded with 10 cloves

METHOD

1 Place everything in a large preserving pan and bring slowly to the boil, it will take some time but stir gently to make sure the sugar doesn't catch.
2 Simmer for about 3 hours, stirring occasionally. It will be a thick dark colour.
3 Pack into sterilised jars and cover. Leave to mature for a couple of months.

Delicious with oatcakes and Anster or St Andrews Farmhouse cheese.

COURGETTE FLOWERS STUFFED WITH MOZZARELLA AND ANCHOVIES

This idea comes from Maria Sisci, a student friend at St Andrews University who is half Chinese and half Italian! Maria's aunt Lilli (on the Italian side!) does these delicious flowers dipped in a light beer batter.

INGREDIENTS

8-12 courgette flowers
Oil for deep frying
(or a deep fat fryer)
Thin slices of mozzarella
Anchovy fillets

75g cornflour
75g plain flour
1 egg
180ml light beer

METHOD

1 Make sure the flowers are dry and then wrap a couple of anchovy fillets around the mozzarella slices and stuff them inside the flowers, twisting the tops lightly to enclose the stuffing.
2 Make the batter by sifting the flours into a bowl and break the egg into the centre whisking gently to incorporate and then enough beer to form a light batter, don't over mix, it's best to have a few lumps!
3 Heat the oil in a deep pan and when hot, dip the flowers into the batter, allow some to pour off then plunge in to the hot oil. Only cook 3 at a time and cook for a couple of minutes.

Drain on kitchen paper and serve sprinkled with sea salt.

SHREDDED COURGETTE

This may not sound much like a recipe! But this most simple of ideas comes from a great cook – John Tovey who ran the legendary Miller Howe hotel in the lake district. Cooking was theatre for him and he always had about 7 different vegetables each night for dinner, this was often one.

INGREDIENTS

450g courgettes
2 limes, zest and juice
50g butter

METHOD

1   Wipe the courgettes, top and tail them and grate finely.
2   Mix with the juice and zest, leave for at least half an hour.
3   In a large frying pan over a high heat melt the butter and as the last bit fizzles and melts throw in the courgettes and cook quickly tossing in the pan to cook evenly, season if necessary.

I sometimes finish this with a splash of Marsala.

COURGETTE AND CABBAGE CRUMBLE

I am still put off by the c word as I have strong memories of overcooked school sludge which stood for cabbage and I couldn't eat cabbage until in my early 20s when I discovered cooking cabbage without water! So don't be put off by this ingredient for this yummy dish! You can either cook it in a dish as suggested below or in individual ramekins as I have done for the picture.

INGREDIENTS

200g cooked rice
4 courgettes thinly sliced
1 cabbage, shredded
2 eggs
400ml full fat milk
200g Anster cheese
Salt and freshly ground black pepper
100g breadcrumbs

METHOD

1   Preheat the oven to 180C gas mark 4.
2   Sauté the courgettes and cabbage in a little butter for a few minutes until soft.
3   Mix the vegetables with the rice.
4   Mix the eggs with the milk and add half the cheese. Mix with the vegetables and season with salt and pepper.
5   Put in an ovenable dish, mix the remaining cheese with bread crumbs and sprinkle on top bake until crisp. About 20 minutes.

TOMATO AND COURGETTE SALAD WITH CUMIN

Another Sybil Kapoor inspired dish. I love the gentle touch with the cinnamon just giving a light eastern flavour to this salad.

INGREDIENTS

3 tblsp olive oil
1 small onion finely chopped
2 cloves garlic crushed with a little sea salt
Pinch smoked sea salt (optional)
½ cinnamon stick
1 tsp ground cumin
6 ripe tomatoes, blanched and peeled (as per ratatouille p37) and diced
6 courgettes cut in rounds or quartered
Pinch sugar
Salt and freshly ground black pepper
1 tblsp chopped parsley

METHOD

1   Heat the oil in a large frying pan and gently soften the onion for a few minutes, stir in the garlic.
2   Add the spices and continue to cook for 5 minutes.
3   Add the tomatoes and increase heat and stir until cooked to a puree.
4   Add the courgettes and cook to colour a little, check for seasoning and remove from heat.
5   Remove the cinnamon stick and allow to cool, serve with brown bread and creamy yoghurt.

COURGETTES SKEWERED WITH LEMON AND CHICKEN

A very simple summer barbecue idea. Lemon and chicken go well together and here I have combined colour and texture to provide a yummy barbecue dish. Serve with salads and maybe some rice or couscous.

INGREDIENTS

650g chicken breasts
3 courgettes
225g button mushrooms
12 cherry tomatoes
Zest and juice of 3 lemons
3 tblsp olive oil
1 tblsp brown sugar
1 tblsp red wine vinegar
1 clove garlic, crushed
1 tsp salt
¼ tsp cayenne

METHOD

1   Cut the chickens into 50 cm chunks and slice the courgettes into 25 cm slices.
2   Thread them alternately on skewers with the button mushrooms and tomatoes, place in a shallow tray.
3   Combine the marinading ingredients,and pour over the skewers and leave at room temperature for a couple of hours.
4   Barbecue quite slowly so that the chicken cooks through but the vegetables aren't burnt!

ROUND COURGETTES STUFFED WITH RED RICE AND VEGETABLES

INGREDIENTS

170g red rice (raw weight), cooked
8 round courgettes
3 tomatoes
2 slices smoked venison (optional)
1 carrot, peeled and cut into
thin strips
3 garlic cloves, chopped
½ an onion, peeled and chopped
Olive oil
1 tsp ground coriander

1 tsp ground cumin
30g aged St Andrews
farmhouse cheese
1 tblsp basil, chopped
1 tblsp tarragon, chopped
1 tblsp parsley, chopped
Salt and freshly ground
black pepper
A splash of chicken stock or
boiling water

METHOD

1 Preheat the oven to 180C/gas 4.
2 Wash the courgettes and slice off the tops. Remove the flesh from the inside, but keep them whole, dice the flesh roughly and set aside.
3 Blanche the tomatoes in boiling water and refresh in cold water and peel them, when completely cold. Remove the seeds and dice roughly.
4 Heat 2 tblsp olive oil in a heavy-based pan. Add the garlic, onion, coriander and cumin. Stir and cook for 5 minutes until soft but not brown. Add the courgette flesh and stir in. Cook for 3 minutes before adding the carrot, stirring and cooking for 3 minutes before adding the tomatoes. Simmer for 5 minutes uncovered.
5 Remove from the heat and add the diced smoked venison (if using), Cheese and herbs. Season with salt and pepper.
6 Add the rice and mix together. Season the whole courgettes with salt and pepper and stuff them with the rice mixture.
7 Place in an oven proof dish with a splash of stock or water at the bottom. Drizzle with olive oil and bake for about 1 hour.

COURGETTE FRITTATA

A simple take on the Spanish tapa, this can be served either hot or cold and is a great picnic standby.

4 new potatoes, cooked
3 courgettes, diced
2 tblsp olive oil
2 spring onions
3 tblsp chopped parsley
6 eggs
75g Anster cheese, grated
Salt and freshly ground black pepper

1   Turn the grill to high.
2   Dice the potatoes and cook in a medium frying pan, to colour a little.
3   Add the courgettes and stir to mix with the potatoes, add the spring onions and cook for a few minutes.
4   Throw in the parsley and mix thoroughly.
5   Beat the eggs together and season with salt and pepper, and pour over the mixture, shaking and stirring lightly to mix well in, reduce the heat and cook until the mixture comes away from the pan base.
6   Sprinkle over the grated cheese and brown under a hot grill.

SWEET AND SOUR PICKLED COURGETTES

Pickling small courgettes is a great way of preserving a summer glut. Eat as you would a pickled gherkin, or use in tartare sauce with grilled fish. Makes 2-3 jars.

INGREDIENTS

450g small courgettes, thickly sliced lengthways
1 tsp salt, plus extra for sprinkling
1 tsp turmeric
2 tsp mustard seeds
2 star anise
2 tblsp clear honey
300ml cider vinegar
10 shallots, sliced into thin rings

METHOD

1   Sprinkle the courgettes with salt and leave for 1 hour.
2   Mix the turmeric, salt, mustard seeds, honey, vinegar and star anise in a pan, bring to the boil and simmer for five minutes. Leave to cool, skimming the surface if necessary.
3   Drain the courgettes, wash well and pat dry. Pack into warmed, clean jars with the shallot rings. Cover with the spiced vinegar. Seal well and store for 2-3 days before eating.

MARINATED COURGETTE SALAD

Use different coloured courgettes for this simple summer salad or a squash can be a good alternative.

INGREDIENTS

8 small courgettes yellow and green, sliced thinly at an angle
2 sticks celery chopped
1 red onion, peeled and thinly sliced, across the grain
1 red pepper quartered, seeded and thinly sliced
4 tblsp sherry vinegar
2 tblsp brown sugar
2 tblsp rapeseed oil
1 tsp sea salt
1 tsp freshly ground black pepper

METHOD

1   Mix all the vegetables together in a bowl.
2   Combine the remaining ingredients in a saucepan and bring to the boil to dissolve the sugar.
3   Pour over the mixed vegetables, and leave to marinate.

Delicious served as an accompaniment to barbecue foods.

CRAB AND COURGETTE BAKE

A simply delicious dish from my great friend David Naylor who has combined crab with the method of making a potato dauphinoise. I have simply changed the cheese.

INGREDIENTS

1 clove of garlic
100ml double cream
3 courgettes, thinly sliced lengthwise
200g St Andrews farmhouse cheese, grated
1 dressed crab

METHOD

1   Turn the oven to 200C gas mark 6.
2   Take a gratin dish and cut the garlic in half and sprinkle in a little salt and rub the garlic all over the base of the dish.
3   Place a layer of courgette on the base season with salt and pepper then sprinkle over some cheese, spread over the crab.
4   Top with the remaining courgette slices, pour over the cream and the remaining cheese.
5   Bake in the oven for 30 minutes until brown and bubbling.

HERB TABOULEH WITH ROASTED COURGETTES

Based on an idea from my visit to the Lebanon in search of a friend's roots Lebanese food is simple but relies on lovely fresh ingredients.

INGREDIENTS

2 courgettes cut into slices
2 tsp plus 2 tblsp summer harvest rapeseed oil
Salt and freshly ground black pepper
125g bulgar wheat
2 plum tomatoes blanched and chopped like ratatouille (page 37)
4 spring onions
150 (half) cucumber, peeled, de-seeded and chopped
1 tblsp chopped flat parsley
1 tblsp chopped mint
Grated zest and juice of a lemon

METHOD

1   Preheat the oven to 220C gas mark 7, toss the courgettes in 2 tsp oil season with salt and pepper and roast in a single layer.
2   Rinse and drain the bulgar wheat and cook in 600ml cold water for 15 minutes until most of the water is absorbed, drain.
3   Add the diced tomatoes, spring onions, cucumber, herbs and pepper to the bulgar wheat.
4   Whisk together the oil, lemon zest and juice and mix through.
5   Place the roasted courgettes on a plate and dress with the tabbouleh.

COURGETTE MUFFINS

served drizzled with honey these make an unusual breakfast dish with good coffee out in the sunshine!

INGREDIENTS

3 eggs
75ml vegetable oil
150ml full fat milk
200g plain flour
1 tsp salt
2 tsp baking powder
100g caster sugar
150g grated courgettes squeezed dry

METHOD

1   Turn the oven to 180C gas mark 6.
2   Beat the eggs with the oil and milk.
3   Mix the flour with the salt baking powder and sugar.
4   Fold the wet mixture in to the dry mixture and lastly gently stir in the courgettes.
5   Pour into 12 muffin moulds and bake for 20 minutes.

BIOGRAPHIES

CAROLINE TROTTER is a freelance photographer and works across a wide variety of subjects. Weddings are her main area of work but she also does portraits, both human and animal – horses, dogs etc. Caroline covers events for associations such as Fife Chamber of Commerce and provides business portraits for websites and marketing purposes. She also runs photography courses from home.

www.carolinetrotter.co.uk

CHRISTOPHER TROTTER is Fife's Food Ambassador, an honorary title bestowed on him for his work promoting food from Fife. He is also a freelance chef, cookery writer and food commentator, appearing on programmes such as BBC radio Scotland's Kitchen café and Kitchen garden. As a consultant he has worked with agencies as diverse as Argyll and the Island's Enterprise and The National Trust for Scotland. Christopher also provides cookery classes and food tours and he is passionate about fresh produce in its season.

www.fifefoodambassador.co.uk

They have two children, one hen (currently), two dogs and a mac cat. And live in rural Fife.

ACKNOWLEDGEMENTS

To create 30 recipes for courgettes has of course involved conversations with friends, going through my own archive of ideas and recipes as well as of course picking up ideas from other cooks, chefs and food writers. Most of my direct sources are acknowledged in these pages but I just want to make some indirect ones here as well.

David Naylor former Sharrow Bay chef always contributes to my thoughts with ideas and e mails and in particular the baked crab idea.

Alison Sykora who is as happy in a galley on a yacht as she is in more usual kitchens gave me the pesto idea.

Thanks to Beth from Forty Hall Farm in Enfield who let me have a male flower from her courgettes for the photo and then gave me the first Courgette they had grown under plastic in May!

It is always good to be able to acknowledge people who inspire you even if their work doesn't appear here. So . . .

. . . thanks to Myrtle Allen, Sybil Kapoor, Nigel Slater, Yotam Ottolenghi, Guy Watson, Jane Baxter. Bruce Bennett of Pillars of Hercules and the wonderful Pollock family and staff from Ardross farm.

ST ANDREWS CHEESE

THE STEWART FAMILY has been farming at Falside Farm in the east of Fife since the 1930s. Today, we run a mixed farming business, growing wheat, barley and oilseed rape, with the dairy at the heart of the business.

Jane started to make cheese in 2008, using the milk from her husband Robert's herd of home bred Friesian Holstein cows. The cows are fed a natural diet including home produced barley, straw and grass silage, and in the summer months they graze the lush pastures overlooking the sea towards Anstruther – the local fishing town from which the cheese takes its name.

Traditional farming methods with careful stockmanship and attention to detail at every stage combine to ensure contented cows, producing top quality raw milk. To this, we add traditional farmhouse cultures, natural rennet, time and care – and a generous measure of enthusiasm! – to produce our award winning artisan cheeses.

Anster is a crumbly farmhouse cheese, with a good level of acidity and a lovely 'lemony' tang on the finish. Delicious in a brown bread sandwich with a fruity pickle such as Trotter's Mostarda, but equally good on its own with a sweet oatmeal biscuit and a glass of cider or a light beer. It has many culinary uses, but it is especially good crumbled into a risotto as a delicious alternative to Parmesan.

Red Anster – the flavour-added 'sister' cheese to Anster – incorporates fresh garlic and fresh chives in the recipe, along with a splash of annatto (natural food colouring). The use of fresh herbs gives a unique characteristic to the cheese – lending savoury notes which conjure up dreams of summer barbecues, grilled meats and tossed salads to tantalise the taste buds.

St Andrews Farmhouse is a mature cheddar style cheese. Aged for 9 months to produce a well rounded flavour and a creamy texture, this cheese definitely punches above its weight for its age. This is the perfect ingredient for a cheese sauce. It is very good melted on toast and served with an onion chutney – or why not enjoy a nibble with a glass of Pinotage.

Awards to date have included Gold at the International Cheese Awards, and a Great Taste Gold Star for Anster; Sliver at the British Cheese Awards for St Andrews Farmhouse; and Gold at the Royal Highland Show for Red Anster.

We are very proud to be part of the resurgence in Scottish farmhouse cheese-making, contributing to the wealth of wonderful produce which Scotland in general – and Fife in particular – has to offer.

Jane Stewart

NOTES